Weird Places

by David Orme

Trailblazers

Weird Places
by David Orme
Educational consultant: Helen Bird

Illustrated by Martin Bolchover and Cyber Media (India) Ltd.

Published by Ransom Publishing Ltd.
Rose Cottage, Howe Hill, Watlington, Oxon. OX49 5HB
www.ransom.co.uk

ISBN   184167 589 X
        978 184167 589 3

First published in 2006

Weird Places

Contents

Get the facts: Weird place files   **5**

File 1:	The Bermuda triangle	6
File 2:	Death Valley	7
File 3:	Loch Ness	8
File 4:	The Himalayas	9
File 5:	Underwater volcanoes	10
File 6:	Uluru	11
File 7:	The Tower of London	12
File 8:	Jungle temples	13
File 9:	Lake Vostok	14
File 10:	Flores Island	15
File 11:	Stonehenge	16
File 12:	Oak Island	17

Fiction

The Lost Tribe   19

Weird places word check   **36**

Weird Places

Get
the
facts

Fact file 1: *The Bermuda triangle*

Where is it?   In the Atlantic Ocean, south of Bermuda.

Amazing facts: Many ships and planes have disappeared here.

In 1945 five planes of 'Flight 19' disappeared.

50 small planes disappeared here between 1978 and 2002. So did many boats.

What is happening?

Is it:

- ◎ Compasses that stop working?
- ◎ Giant gas bubbles from the bottom of the sea?
- ◎ **ALIENS?**

The coastguards say:

- ◎ The sea is dangerous here.
- ◎ Too many sailors are not well trained.
- ◎ Boats often get lost at sea.

WHAT DO YOU THINK?

Fact file 2: **Death Valley**

Where is it?   California, USA.

Amazing facts: Death Valley is below the level of the sea.

It is one of the *hottest* places in the world. The record in the valley is 56.7 °C (134 °F).

It does not rain much in Death Valley. But when it does there can be dangerous floods.

Animals like rattlesnakes and scorpions have adapted to live there.

The Timbisha tribe of Native Americans have lived there for over 1,000 years.

If you go to Death valley:

- Take plenty of water.
- Don't play with the rattlesnakes
- Don't forget the sun cream!

Rattlesnake – not friendly!

Fact file 3: *Loch Ness*

Where is it?	Scotland, U.K.
Amazing facts:	People say there is a monster living in the loch. It looks like a dinosaur.

But:

The water is too cold for a reptile-like a dinosaur.

There aren't enough fish in the loch to feed a big animal.

WHAT DO YOU THINK?

The most famous picture of Nessie is

— **A FAKE!**

Fact file 4: *The Himalayas*

Where are they?   In the countries of Nepal, Tibet and India.

Amazing facts: The Himalayas are the highest mountains in the World. More than 30 of the mountains are higher than 7,600 metres.

The highest mountain in the rest of the world is less than 7,000 metres high.

Himalaya means 'place of snow'.

Weird facts

People say that a creature called the Yeti lives in the Himalayas.

They have found red fur.

Do you believe in the Yeti?

They have seen giant footprints.

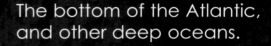

Fact file 5: *Underwater volcanoes*

Where are they?

The bottom of the Atlantic, and other deep oceans.

They are sometimes called black smokers.

Amazing facts:

At the bottom of the ocean there is no light or oxygen.

Many creatures still manage to live here.

They get their food from the chemicals the volcanoes give out.

Some scientists think that this is how life started on Earth.

Fact file 6: Uluru

Where is it? In the centre of Australia. It is also called Ayers Rock.

Amazing facts: Uluru is in the middle of a huge desert.

The rock is over 300 metres high and 8 km round.

As the light changes through the day the rock changes colour

Many strange animals live here.

Red Kangaroo

A Goanna lizard

A holy place

Uluru is a holy place for native Australians.

11

Fact file 7: The Tower of London

Where is it?　　London,
　　　　　　　　　　England.

Amazing facts:　The first tower
　　　　　　　　　　was built nearly
　　　　　　　　　　1,000 years ago.

Thousands of people have been locked up, tortured, executed and murdered there.

Weird facts

In 1815 a guard saw the ghost of a bear. He stabbed it and the bear disappeared. A few days later, the guard was dead!

A man with an axe has been seen chasing a screaming woman!

Why do people say the Tower of London is haunted?

◎ **because it really is?**

◎ **because it makes more people come and visit it?**

What do you think?

Fact file 8: *Jungle temples*

Where can I find them?

Jungle temples are found all around the world.

This temple is at Tikal, in Guatemala, in Central America.

History

The Mayan people lived in Tikal for 1,000 years. They left in 800 AD.

It was lost and covered by jungle. It was not found again until the 19th century.

Weird facts

Tikal has a ball court where they played a game like football. It is said that the losers became human sacrifices!

The temple was used in the film Star Wars.

Fact file 9: *Lake Vostok*

Where is it? In Antarctica.

Amazing facts: Lake Vostok is huge
– about the same size as
Lake Ontario in Canada.

It was found in 1996. It is under 4,000 metres of ice.

This water has been sealed off from the air for millions of years.

Scientists are drilling through the ice to find out what is in Lake Vostok.

There could be living things down there – but they will probably be very tiny.

The drilling isn't easy – Vostok station is the coldest place on Earth!

Vostok station

Fact file 10: Flores Island

Where is it?

South East Asia.

Amazing facts:

Keli Mutu is a volcano with three lakes. Each lake has a different colour.

Two of the world's rarest animals can be found here, the Flores giant rat and the Komodo dragon (*left*).

An amazing discovery

In 2004 scientists found the skeletons of tiny humans, just 1 metre tall. These people lived on the island 18,000 years ago.

Local people say a tribe of little people called Ebu Gogo died out 200 years ago.

Could a tribe of tiny humans still be living on an unexplored island?

Fact file 11: *Stonehenge*

Where is it? Wiltshire, U.K.

Amazing facts: Stonehenge was started over 5,000 years ago.

The builders worked on it for over 2000 years!

Some stones were brought all the way from Wales, using sledges and boats. The biggest stones weigh 40 tons.

How did the builders move them and get them in the right place?

We still don't really know what it was for. People say it was

What do you think?

◎ a temple.

◎ a giant computer.

◎ a place to sacrifice people

Fact file 12: *Oak Island*

Where is it?   Nova Scotia, Canada.

Amazing facts: On the east of the island is the famous **money pit**.

It is said to be the place where pirates hid their loot hundreds of years ago.

The money pit was cleverly made. There are links to the sea. When people try and dig down, the pit fills with water.

Many people have lost their money and their lives trying to find the treasure.

Oak Island in 1931

SEEKING CAPTAIN KIDD'S TREASURE OAK ISLAND CHESTER N.S

Has any treasure been found?

A few pieces of gold chain were found in 1849 – and that's all!

The
Lost
Tribe

Chapter 1:
We're in trouble!

"We're going down!"

Ted Crane and Mike Stone were in trouble. They were travelling around the World in a hot air balloon. Bad weather hit over the Indian Ocean. The balloon was damaged.

Mike sent out a radio message for help but there was no reply.

"Look! An island!"

Below was an island covered with rainforest. Landing there would be better than falling into the sea.

It was a rough landing, but the trees broke their fall. The two men were thrown around the tiny cabin as they hit the ground with a crash.

Chapter 2:
We've got company

"Are you OK Ted?"

"I've hurt my wrist. Think I might have broken it. What about you?"

"I'm O.K. Let's get out of here."

They climbed out of the cabin. It was hot and gloomy under the trees. They could hear the sounds of insects and birds.

Mike had brought the first aid kit. He put a sling round Ted's neck.

"Doesn't look too bad, Ted."

"It hurts like hell. What about a rescue?"

"I don't know if the message got through. The radio is smashed now. They ought to be able to find us. The balloon is easy to see from the air."

Ted put the finger of his good hand to his lips.

"Looks like we've got company," he whispered. Over there. Are they animals?"

They weren't animals. They were people. But Ted and Mike had never seen people like that before.

Chapter 3:
Quite friendly

There were six of them, all male. They had spears. One had two dead animals over his shoulder that looked like big rats.

None of the men was over a metre tall.

They didn't point their spears at Ted and Mike. That was a good start. But they looked surprised to see them. They talked in a language Ted and Mike didn't know.

"Who the heck are these tiny people?" asked Ted.

"Didn't you read about the skeletons they found on Flores Island?"

"But they have been dead for 18,000 years!"

"Well, this lot aren't dead. In fact, they look quite friendly!"

Ted and Mike tried to look friendly too. They didn't want to be prodded by a spear!

Chapter 4:
Achoo!

The little men took Ted and Mike to a huge cave nearby. More little people were there.

The giant rats were thrown on to a fire. Ted and Mike were given the best bit to eat – the heads!

"This is disgusting," whispered Mike.

"Tastes better than stuff from our local burger bar," replied Ted.

One of the men looked at Ted's wrist. He went into the cave and came back with some dried leaves. He wrapped them round the wrist.

"Amazing," said Ted. "The pain's gone away!"

Mike sneezed loudly. The people jumped up in alarm. They had never seen anyone sneeze before!

"I wonder if that guy has got anything to cure my cold," said Mike.

Then they heard a sound in the sky. A helicopter!

The little people rushed to hide. Mike waved and the helicopter dropped a rope. Soon they were safely in the helicopter.

Weeks later, a ship came to the island. Scientists had heard Ted and Mike's story. They wanted to see the little people for themselves.

But they were too late. Mike's cold had spread to the little people. It was a new disease for them.

The Ebu Gogo were dead.

Weird places word check

adapted

aboriginals

balloon

chemical

coastguard

compass

creature

disappeared

drilling

executed

helicopter

human

human sacrifice

loch

monster

mountain

murdered

native

Native American

Native Australian

ocean

pirate

rattlesnake

reptile

rarest

rescue

scientist

scorpion

sealed off

temperature

tortured

trained

tribe

unknown

volcano